Treasures of Life 1

The Daily Devotional

By Shelley Teig

I would love to hear from you.

www.goodlifebooks.com
goodlifebooks18@gmail.com

Edited by John Ivaska, Gail Smith, Kim Hutter, Kathy Elliott,
Melinda Prince and Martin Teig
This book is printed in the U.S.A.

ISBN 9781537464541

About the Author:

Shelley was born in Iowa. She lived in a small town of Parkersburg, IA. At the tender age of seven, she and her sister, Elaine answered an alter call together to ask our wonderful Savior in their hearts. It was there she knew things would not be the same. She has a partner for life from now on. With Jesus and the Holy Spirit, she decided to get baptized at the age of 11. In her teenage years, she went on a mission trip with a youth group to Colorado. In this setting of ministry and daily devotional time, she began to hunger for the word of God.

In 1980, she married Martin, and they have three children: Amanda, Adreane and Caleb. They moved to Ozark, MO in 1993. Shelley was a stay at home mom. After much thought, she took on home schooling their children which began at tenth, eighth,.and second grade. With this new challenge, she asked for wisdom, strength, and the leading of the Holy Spirit. As she was staying at home, her entrepreneurial husband started a wheel chair company with a partner. On one side of an oversized warehouse a ministry called the Launch Pad was started. They shipped 4 million pounds of food, clothing, medical supplies all over the world and locally. Many families came to help in this endeavor as well as Shelley and their children.

After raising their children in a christian environment and learning to let them go, Shelley began to work for Integrity Home Heath Care over the summer until home schooling their last child was complete. Shelley and her husband, Martin, remodeled many of their homes as well as helped their pastor start up the Healing River International Ministry as well as the school of ministry. While being involved in leadership and prophetic ministry training she, started writing this devotional book. In the pursuit for an investment, they bought a laundromat, which they later turned into a furniture and craft store and then offices that helped them start their investment portfolio. Shelley became a Realtor for about four years while she and her husband began to buy, remodel, and invest in residential and resort real estate and a campground.

Forward

So much of the time in the current atmosphere of Christianity, we have complicated our walk with the Lord. Shelley Teig has been able to bring profound truths in an easy to understand way so that the follower of Christ can truly grow in His grace and mercy. We believe that anyone who will take the time to make this devotional a part of their daily walk will experience growth and encouragement and their journey.

Mitch and Gail Smith

Pastors, Kulm Assembly of God

Endorsement

I am pleased to recommend this book by Shelley Teig. The Kingdom principles contained within its pages are from a life that has lived them out on a daily basis. I personally know that Shelley thinks, talks, and acts with the leading of the Holy Spirit. It has become very natural for her to let the flow of the Spirit affect her daily life, and now she shares the benefits she has learned with her readers.

John Ivaska

Table of Contents

Introduction

My mission statement is to captivate you with your walk with God. May Jesus bless your life as you read and grow stronger in Him!

Many of us have challenges in life. Some have been lessons we have learned along the way.

I wish to tell everybody about the lessons I've learned. They have been in times of tears and joy for me. Some moments require wisdom from the Most High God, my Heavenly Father. He has given me my answers. All I have to do is ask the Holy Spirit for direction. In fact, I owe my whole life for such a friendship. In that friendship, He has never let me down. I have had some divine times with Him in a personal relationship with Jesus. Sometimes I say things to people I will never see again. The moments go by so fast. I wish I could talk to everyone. I just want people to understand my heart. This is the reason I have developed this devotional series with a glimpse of my challenges and hopes, as well as His revelations to me. Please enjoy it. Maybe just one thing that is in it will change your life or destiny! Please read it every day! Also share with a friend that it may help alter their life as well.

Day 1 - Finding the Way

Romans 3:10-26; 5:6-20; 10:8-15

When you you look at this earth, you see the creations that God has given us to enjoy. This reminds me that He is coming back again. People that don't look forward to His coming need an awakening. Nobody knows when He will return to this earth. The best thing to do is to be ready. On this first page, I wanted to give you a chance to know Jesus Christ as your Savior. It's time for you to take that stand with Him. He knows that you need to be a partner with Him. When he died on the cross it was a gift. You can't be good enough to come to Father God without Jesus' gift of life for you. We all have sinned, but Jesus' death paid for our sin by His own blood on that cross. If you are serious about taking a step of faith say this prayer. "Dear Jesus I want you as my Savior. Lord I receive your gift. I ask you to forgive all my sins and make me clean inside. Thank you for doing this in me today. I would like to be the first one to welcome you into the Kingdom of God. You are now my new sister or brother in Christ Jesus.

After you have taken that step, it's time to tell others. Tell them the Love that you have in Christ. It is the best thing you could ever do! Welcome to the family!

Day 2 - Oh No, Trouble!

James 1:2-6

Have you ever thought, "What do I do when trouble comes?" I have. First, you find out what the trouble is. Sometimes trouble can be from bad choices. Some trouble can be old car parts. What about your physical worn-out bodies? Sometimes consequences of our body stress can causes us trouble. Regardless of what your trouble is, your answer is to praise Jesus anyway. James 1:2-6 says to be joyful in our trials and to ask the Holy Spirit for wisdom. It seems when you praise the Lord, it helps to bring you into the right frame of mind. It also makes our problems look small when we are focused on the creator of the universe. Praise makes our enemy be defeated. Psalm 22:3 says, "Yet you are enthroned as the Holy One; you are the Praise of Israel." God inhabits the praises of his people. If His Spirit is in you, you will have the victory!

Keep on praising the breakthrough will always come.

Day 3 - Passion

Matthew 6:24

When God begins to pour His Spirit on you, you are in the soaking stage. He will pour in you until you are overflowing. Your passion will rise up in you so you can to give it away. We all need the constant pouring in so our overflow from Him can pour back out. We will say to the Lord, "Use me." The Lord will take you up on that. Many times God gives us assignments that we may ignore. We might ignore it because it requires effort, time, and energy. Sometimes God will test our obedience. During times when God has something specific for you to do, He will bring it up again. He will pour into you again and again until you are bursting with His presence. I never dreamed of writing books. My typing skill needs improvement. It's not my passion to sit and type. My passion is to equip the saints and to feed the sheep.

Let your passion go beyond your limitations into His expectations. His passion is in you. He is waiting for willing vessels. He will amaze you with what He can do through you. All you need to do is just let Him out.

Day 4 – How are you Talking?

Ephesians 4:22-32

Some in the body of Christ suffer from what comes out of our mouths. The first trigger to this is usually jealousy, with anger and bitterness following close behind. Slander and gossip often follow jealousy, anger, and bitterness. Verse 29 says, "Do not let any unwholesome talk come out of your mouth, but only what is helpful for building others up according to their needs, that it may benefit those who listen." Unwholesome talk can destroy a church body. Before we talk about someone, let's check our own heart. Is jealousy anger, or bitterness a part of it? Deal with it in prayer and forgiveness as commanded. Then apply kindness and compassion because slander and gossip can can't live in that environment.

Let the words we speak be sweeter than honey!

Day 5 - Can I Change Others?

1 Peter 3:8 -16

We all have been irritated by others actions. Some things that may bother us, are areas in life that bring out our flesh nature. You know, when somebody jokes about you personally, and you think it's not funny at all. It might be the way they act, or their nature just rubs us the wrong way. Some people's habits can really get to us. There are also the times people bother us on purpose. It's the old, "see if I can push your button" game.

I have good news on changing them! Ready, here it is...it all starts with us. We change them by how we respond to them. This takes being humble. Verse 9 says, "Do not repay evil for evil, or insult for insult." Verse 10 says, "... to keep your tongue from evil and your lips from deceitful speech." Verse 11 says, "He must turn from evil and do good and he must seek peace and pursue it." Change comes in by seeking peace and pursuing it. That is what will greatly affect others.

Have you tried to affect others lately by how you speak to them in love? Let's use wisdom in how we speak!

Day 6 - Jesus, that Powerful Name

Colossians 1:15-20

The spiritual realm is just as alive and well as our natural realm. If we could just see the spiritual realm, it would make us aware of the power God has given us. If you want to see a great example read on.

The Lord open my spiritual eyes one evening during a worship service at church. Wow, it was amazing to see the warfare going on. I saw the demons fighting us, and as we worshiped they lost their strength. One thing in particular that I saw, was what happened to the demons when the name of Jesus was shouted. I saw them cringe and cover their ears. I observed them curling up in a little ball with no defense. We are able to stomp on them, and then they were gone. Wow, the powerful name of Jesus.

Let's use that powerful name of Jesus and take dominion and authority the way He wants us to!

Day 7 - What Are You Depending On?

Jeremiah 17: 5-10

Depending on your flesh nature for strength usually has its negative consequences. People who do that often feel like they do not need the Lord. When you let the Holy Spirit do the work, you will learn that trusting in the Lord will bring His strength. Because of the times that we are living in, we need to be closer to the Lord. Verse 8 says, "He will be like a tree planted by the water that sends out its roots by the stream. It does not fear when heat comes; it's leaves are always green. It has no worries in the year of drought and never fails to bear fruit." We are blessed when we rely on the Holy Spirit for our strength and revelation. Think about it

---

Let's listen to to the Holy Spirit often and let Him guide our path!

Day 8 - Our Words Have Power

Proverbs 18:11

I have discovered in my life that words have power. The Lord taught me this lesson in a very supernatural way. A friend gave me some drinking glasses that she didn't want. As she gave me the glasses she said, "I always break glasses, and they will not last at my house." I said, "Thank you, I hardly ever break glasses." I returned home and put the pretty glasses in my top cabinet on the second shelf.

One day one of my glasses took a nose dive out of the second shelf and landed on the hard tile floor. As I saw it falling, I was getting ready for the glass to shatter. To my amazement the glass bounced and spun around and flipped several times. I picked it up off the floor and just looked at it. I could not find a chip or crack on the delicate glass. Then the Holy Spirit spoke to me I remembered saying, "I hardly ever break glasses." Wow! The power of the spoken word. Now that doesn't give us the right to do, and say, foolish things. Just remember to speak positive things. It will help you in many ways. Maybe you won't break glasses either

---

Your words have power, so let's speak the right things out of our mouths!

Day 9 - Breath of Life

Genesis 2:7; John 20:19-23

I was having a conversation with the Father one morning, and, I was thinking and talking about the communication I have with Him. I was thinking how breathing is essential to living. He showed me that is the way we need to walk out our lives. How long can you live if you don't have His breath? We need to breathe His breath every day. We need to take Him with us everywhere we go. Take Him to work. Take Him when you play. Take Him when you're with the kids. His life in us should be like breathing.

Let Him breath in you the breath of life!

Day 10 - Writing on the Wall

Daniel 5

God knows how to get our attention! Nebuchadnezzar was very afraid of the writing on the wall. His face turned pale, his knees knocked together, and his legs gave away. In Nebuchadnezzar's situation, God began to communicate to him in many ways even before the writing on the wall. He even had Daniel interpret the dream before he wrote on the wall. God used a dramatic measure to get his attention because he stopped listening.

Has God tried to communicate to you lately? Are you ignoring His plans? It is helpful to have a place in your spirit to listen to what He is saying to you. He wants an everyday experience with you. We need to be able to talk to Him about our details. Talking to the Lord is not the only thing we need to do. Listening to Him and doing what He says is the other part. Hopefully you will never have the handwriting on the wall experience.

Always keep your spiritual ears on!

Day 11 - Power of Love

1 Corinthians 13

Do you realize that love is a power tool? It is also one of the fruits of the Spirit. In fact, in verse 13, it says that it's the greatest gift. Love also covers a multitude of sin. Operating in love requires forgiveness. It covers sins when you forgive them in love. Jesus' love covers our sin with His own blood and washes us white. Have you noticed how hard it is for someone to fight when you apply love? In Proverbs 25:21-22 says, "If your enemy is hungry, give him food to eat; if he is thirsty, give him water to drink. In doing this, you will heap burning coals on his head, and the Lord will reward you." It means love melts the heart. They can't stand it. It will break their defenses. They seem to just melt in love.

So use your power tool of love, and watch it work for you. You will see hearts melt!

Day 12 - Open Your Heart

Proverbs 15:13-15

Do you know people who have had their hearts closed off? It's difficult for me because I care for them so much. I want to see them set free. When we build up walls we limit God's power. It's not His limitations but ours. We are limiting what we receive from Him. He is such a loving and giving Father, but we can cut off the flow of His blessing.

Those of you who have kids know how much you want your children to do right things. You can reward them, and sometimes you have to discipline them. It's always the Father's heart to reward rather than discipline, both are acts of love. Rewards are so much better than discipline anyway. When you have a wall up, you have a closed heart, which makes it hard to receive anything from your Heavenly Father. Your prospective is off causing you to feel like you are being disciplined. If this is you, your Father wants to touch you today. Remember the rewards are just waiting for you.

Open your heart tear-down the walls and be free!

Day 13 - Money, Money

1 Timothy 6:6-10

It seems like we all need this thing called money. Even Jesus needed money. Remember the coin that Jesus told them to get from the fish's mouth? He needed that to pay taxes.

Have you ever been angry because money seems to control what you could or couldn't do? I know what it feels like when you want to go on a mission trip but can't because of the lack of money. Have you ever seen the poor and wanted to give more than what you have? I believe God wants us to be good stewards of our time and money.

Wisdom and money can make more money if you are willing to take the appropriate steps to learn. Some people need to be taught from mentoring, or from books. Some need to learn how to earn money on their own. In every situation I have learned to use wisdom in giving to the needy. I have seen people who want a big hand out rather than work and support themselves. I believe in teaching people to fish rather than just giving them fish. This is important because it can effect their ability to do their part rather then rely on other people.

So be wise in your giving, and learn to know the why and how to give! Always be obedient what the Lord says to do!

Day 14 - First Love

Luke 14:25-27; Matthew 17:1-9

God has given us the things on this earth. It is good to enjoy God's creation. He is a loving Father who desires for us to see Him as our Creator. Some have worshiped the creation but not the Creator. The world becomes their first love that is more important then Him. When you have a deep desire for the Lord, the things of this world are captured in your heart a different way. He becomes your first love.

In Matthew 17:1-9, some of his disciples had an experience that brought them to a new place in the spiritual realm with Jesus. Jesus lead them into that mountaintop experience where He was transformed. His face shone like the sun and His clothes became white as light. Moses and Elijah were talking with Jesus. Father God was so proud of His Son and wanted them to listen to Him. What happened next was so awesome as the glory cloud came. It shook them to the core, and they fell on their faces being very afraid. When you experience a mountaintop experience, things are different. Your passion becomes so deep.

It's time to go deeper and let the Holy Spirit reveal a fresh newness in your life.

Day 15 - Addictions

1 Peter 5:6-9

Many addictions can begin as a result of the hurt and pain we receive in life. But rather then deal with pain, people have a tendency to bring on addictions. Later in life the pain can be healed, but the addiction can still be left to deal with. Unhealthy habits can be hard to overcome without the grace of God. As I was pondering on the problems of addiction, the Holy Spirit began to enlighten me on the subject. One thing He told me was that people treat an addiction as a friend. It really needs to become their enemy. They cozy up to it in the middle of their stress, and instead of running away from their temptation, they embrace it. I have found out that we need to tap into some wisdom. We are to look for the way out of the temptation. We need to treat the addiction like an enemy. The Bible says to resist the enemy, and he will flee from you. I know you can rise up and overcome this enemy with the help of the Holy Spirit. It's time to say, "I can do all things through Christ which strengthens me" (Phil. 4:13).

Do it today! I believe you will feel better when you do. Take each day one day at a time.

Day 16 - What's Up with Healing?

Isaiah 53:1-5

The subject of healing can be so controversial. As we read in verse five, we find that by Jesus' wounds we are healed. Some translations say we were healed. Healing was there at the cross. It's past tense. The problem comes when we make it present tense. We may say, "If it's your will, please heal me." Just looking at this verse we can see it is His will for us to be healed.

I know sickness isn't something we are supposed to keep. In the Old Testament God used sickness against the wicked. In the New Testament Jesus did everything that was in his Father's will, which included healing people. Because of these miracles, many people believed for their healing when Jesus was around. However, He could only heal a few people in His own town. It was because of doubt and unbelief that stopped them from receiving. The problem is in our ability to receive. Jesus has always healed me anytime I have been sick or injured. First, I knew it was His will for me to be healed. Second, I knew that Jesus had already paid the price for my healing.

Let's say, "Jesus, I receive my healing that my Heavenly Father wants me to have. I resist any form of doubt and unbelief. Thank you for paying the price for me."

Day 17 - Are You Watching?

Mark 13:5-37

There are a lot of studies on the end times. Many scriptures in the gospels tell of the signs that will occur before Jesus' return, but we just don't know exactly when that will happen. I think we always need to be ready for Jesus' return. It's so important that He told us to watch and pray and be on alert! To always be on guard. Have you ever thought, "This could be the day?"

I have met a lot of Christians in my life. Some tell me that they are Christian, but their actions tell me different. Jesus said that we would know them by their love for one another. Jesus also stated that if we love Him we would keep His Commandments. One of the best ways to be ready for His return is to love one another, and always obey the Lord.

Let's all be ready and watching!

Day 18 - Restoring Honor

Isaiah 8:11-17; Deuteronomy 5:16; 6:5

Today people in our society have a "no fear" mentality. We have a game show where people go to the extreme to show they have no fear. Some fear, however, is good. The fear the of Lord is good. The fear of the Lord is made up of respect, honor, adoration, and worship to our Creator. We don't take the name of the Lord in vain if we have proper respect and honor. Honor and respect should be given to our Heavenly Father as well as our earthly father.

In Deuteronomy it talks about honoring your father and your mother. Why should we honor our parents? So things can go well and have a long life on the earth. One thing I see in our society is a lack of honor and respect. You might be thinking, "My dad treats me bad. So how can I honor him if he does wrong things?" The secret of respect is to love the person and hate the sin. Separate all the bad things but love that person. Your Heavenly Father also wants your respect and honor too! Maybe you are mad at God. Separate all the bad thoughts you have. Now love Him with everything you have! He is your loving Father.

Let's return to honor and respect and see what will happen.

Day 19 - Are Your Prayers Blocked?

1 John 3:19-24; 5:14-16; 1 Peter 3:1-12

Have you ever wondered if your prayers are being answered? There are some things we can do to make sure they are effective. First we need to make sure our heart is pure. In verse 22, it talks about obeying His commandments and doing what pleases Him. Second, you should pray the will of God. We can pray for a lot of things, but how many pray for His will? In 1 John 5:14-16, it talks about how the Lord hears us if we pray His will. Pray God's word, for His will is in the word. Another point is for praying husbands 1 Peter 3:7 says, "Husbands, in the same way be consecrated as you live with your wives, and treat them with respect as the weaker partner and as heirs with you of the gracious gift of life, so that nothing will hinder your prayers." There are many things that can get in the way of our prayers, but these are the three I think can be overlooked.

May your prayers be an effective tool in the hands of our King!

Day 20 - Dancing with Joy

Psalm 149:1-9

I love worshiping the Lord! It's also fun to dance to the Lord! David even danced his outer garments off, his worship was one of the reasons why God called David the apple of his eye. I also believe it was because he deeply repented of his sins and really loved God with his whole heart.. He ministered to the Lord in his worship. Father God likes us to worship with everything we have. When we worship, let's do it to please our Father. Ask the Father to give you the heart of worshiping Him in anyway He would want you to. Remember, worship is to Him and not to other people. He created us to worship Him.

Do it today and let Joy fill your heart!

Day 21 - Comfort Indeed

Acts 2:1-21

Although my mother wasn't a smoker, she passed away from cancer in 2006. After five months of praying for my mother's healing, the Lord told me two things. My pet bird, Tweety, was going to die and then my mom. The Lord wanted to prepare me ahead of time, and they were both gone six weeks later.

Looking back, I will never forget what happened on the day of my mom's death. We were on our way to Iowa when I received a phone call at 6:00 P.M. It was my dad saying my mom had passed away. We were in the middle of Missouri at the time. After receiving that news, I began to weep deeply. I tried to rest, but my mind was on what had happened. I knew people were praying for us. Suddenly right in our Jeep the Holy Spirit, as the comforter, showed up. Wow! My Heavenly Father's love permeated my very being, and I had great peace. This had such an impact on me.

The disciples when they had to wait for the Comforter to come after Jesus' death. Can you imagine how awesome that day was? They saw and felt things different than before. Today that same Comforter is here.

He will get you through the valleys of your life. Let Him give you comfort an peace today!

Day 22 - Religious Pride and Arrogance

Romans 12

Think about all the people who love the Lord. Denominations may seem to divide us, but In reality, we are all part of the body of Christ. I have attended churches in different areas, and one thing that I saw, was their love for Jesus and for one another. Those that love Jesus have a shine upon them, and you can sense and feel their passion for the Lord. It will spill out of them and on to others. Many churches can be different in style, music, form, programs, and a lot of other things. I have my preferences, and I'm sure you do too. One of the things that the Holy Spirit begin to teach me is to watch out for religious pride that says, "My church does things the right way." It can also sound like, "that church doesn't know as much as we do," or, "you can sure feel the Holy Spirit here more than over at that other church." It is time for repentance if this has been in your heart. Don't think more highly of yourself. Learn to love the things that the Father loves. He loves His people who love Him and seek Him. We need to see all churches in the eyes of our Father. It will include His love for other brothers and sisters in the body of Christ. We all are to become the bride of Christ.

Let's guard against the religious pride that can occur so quickly in us. Ask the Holy Spirit to fill you with the love of the Father and to be humble.

Day 23 - Frustration or Trust

Proverbs 34; Psalm 25

We all go through times of disappointments, when life seems to throw us around. Some of us fight back, but others give up and become depressed. So to ease the pain, erratic behavior addictions may come into their lives.

I have learned to take the punches and get back up. One thing I know, is to always go to my Heavenly Father for help. He has brought me through storm after storm. I have learned every storm at the time looks like a big huge mountain, but after a year they all look a lot smaller. Looking back I'm remembering His faithfulness and that He was always there for me.

Some people think that things have to turn out a certain way. Have you ever put in your request and things went exactly opposite? That can be frustrating, but it is also when trust comes in. Go beyond the moment of your problems and trust Him. It may help to speak out that you are trusting Him, declaring scriptures of trust. I know it will pay off in the end, and He will give you peace. You will be able to look back and see His faithfulness. It's not on your own power to do this.

Let Him guide you in His strength. Trust Him! It feels so good!

Day 24 - Purpose and Toning Up

Philippians 3:12-16

Purpose can be the key to doing what God wants you to do, and it can be a process. Have you ever seen a weight lifter? They lift weights to build up their muscle tone. Physically you have to get ready for whatever that weight might be. Could you run ten miles a day if you were out of shape? Of course not. Usually you would tone up first by starting with a half a mile the first week or two. Then you may do a mile the next two weeks until you're ready for the ten miles.

Think and pray in your spirit about your purpose and destiny. You need to tone up and get ready for what God has for you to do. Think back in your life. Have you grown spiritually? Have you been toning up for your purpose? If not, it is time to start. Be spiritually prepared for when your purpose calls on you by the Lord. If you are wondering why you can't seem to get going on the things God wants you to do, then your Heavenly Father may have you spiritually working out.

Be ready and stay purposed in whatever state you might be in! And tone those spiritual muscles!

Day 25 - Marking Your Heart

Luke 9:57-62

Have you ever had God put a bulls-eye on your heart? That bulls-eye target is something that He really wants you to do or understand. I have, and when He did, it left a lasting impression. It will bring a change if you don't ignore it. Sometimes I have ignored the bulls-eye. I have found that when He had something for me to do He would often bring it back around. We all have choices to close or open our heart to the bulls-eye. However, there is a difference in ignoring a bulls-eye and preparing for it. Everyone knows it takes change when God does a work in us, big or small. We need His heart to take us to a new level called commitment. Bulls-eye time, and commitment bring accomplishment, and the stability we need in the hard places. Do you want to be stable and able to remain faithful in the hard times? Then just keep pressing through.

Let Him put the bulls-eye on you. You will be able to accomplish what he needs you to do. Ask Father God to mark your heart today!

Day 26 - Purity in Prosperity

Psalm 1; 2 Corinthians 9:6-10

Not everything you see in the realm of the Spirit is pure. Fellow believers can be led in the wrong way. Having money isn't bad, but having the wrong motive of the heart is. You can be rich or poor, and still money can have control of you becoming its slave. Some have used the wrong mindset in wealth building. Rather than being a "taker," you need to be a "giver" of yourself to others.

I know what it was like to serve my Lord and lack the resources I needed. The Father wants to give us the plans to prosper us. He wants to teach us good financial principles. Some people are so controlled by money that they spend it all and don't save to invest. In that way money, becomes their God. The big desire of "I want it now" is strong in a lot of people, but to discipline your spending and save to invest is wisdom. To prosper, the Bible says, to give and you will receive. Increasing your seed money frees you to give and have provision to do the things God wants you to do. You don't need to ask others for that money but can give it away. Let go and trust Him!

Ask the Father for wisdom in investing and He will show you how! Let the Holy Spirit teach you to be a good responder to purity in prosperity!

Day 27 - Doors of Opportunities

Romans 8:1-16

How do you respond when things don't go your way? I have to admit, my feathers can get ruffled at times. Early in life, we all find out that things don't go our way. Sometimes we have to ask ourselves, "Am I acting like a spoiled child?" Maturity comes with age; however, I have seen many adults act like spoiled children. Usually we get bent out of shape because we have a hard time with challenges.

During the Exodus the children of Israel were led by fire at night and cloud during the day. We are led by the Holy Spirit and our Heavenly Father. We get bent out of shape when we are not listening to the Holy Spirit and doing what is right. Righteousness is found in the heart that is open to the Holy Spirit. Doing the right thing opens the doors of opportunities for God's glory to shine in us. It's comforting to know when things change we can move with that change led by the Spirit.

Move with the Holy Spirit. Let him be your guide through your life of change.

Day 28 - Mighty in His Kingdom

2 Corinthians 5:1-10

Have you ever felt worn out and tired of everything? I'm sure we all get this way. One thing I do know, when I feel that way is because I haven't ask for strength from Him. So often we attempt to go on mere human strength. I think what happens is we get so caught up in the natural world we live in.

We are really busy people. Things can easily get attached to our "to do" list. Then the world and pressure seem to press in on us to defeat us, and we find we can't go on our own human strength. These problems just sneak up on us with recurring frequency.

Here are some things to help. (1) Stop and look at the spiritual realm. (2) Listen to the voice of the Father through the Holy Spirit. (3) Change the course of action if any is needed. (4) Focus on what the Bible says. (5) Declare you are a mighty man or woman of valor. (6) Take your stand and be seated in heavenly places in Christ Jesus.

You can take charge of any situation with help of the Father through the Holy Spirit! Be mighty in His Kingdom in all areas of your life!

Day 29 - Fly Away Butterfly

Proverbs 17:6

My heart is tender towards family life. I know when you have children, life can get busy. You spend a lot of time with them, so you get used to them being around. When our girls left home, our son was sixteen. He had a Jeep so he was constantly coming and going. I was beginning to experience that empty nest feeling.

For our 26th wedding anniversary on Easter, we went to Big Cedar Lodge. As I observed all the families together, my heart sank as I remembered back to the days when my kids were still at home. February 26th mom died, which didn't help either. I was grieving.

Later that I decided to burn some branches. I saw a beautiful butterfly fluttering in the ashes, so I reached my hand down. Suddenly, It flew and went over my neighbors house and disappeared. Then my Heavenly Father spoke to me and said that I needed to let my butterflies (my children) fly away too. He will watch over them. I realized that my memories of family life were like ashes, and my children needed to make their own life and memories.

The Holy Spirit helps you through the empty nest syndrome as they fly away as that butterfly. He will take them.

Day 30 - Live and Die

Philippians 1:27-26

Losing my mom was a hard thing to experience. I felt like I had to be the strong one in the family after her death. I was able to stay with my dad about three weeks after she was gone. During that time we were busy cleaning, which didn't allow much grieving time. My sister also stayed to help clean out all the mystery drawers, closets, and spare bedrooms that held mom's treasures and projects. It was quite an adventure.

Afterwards it was good to return home. I began to unpack some of the things I had brought back from dads, and that is when my grieving started. I didn't realize that I had tucked my emotions deep down inside me. Grieving is a natural thing, and those of you who lost a loved one need to grieve. It will not hurt you, but will help release your emotions connected with that person. If you don't grieve properly, it will lock your emotions up as you push it down in your subconscious mind. Grieving helps you let go of the person and will heal your heart.

Don't always try to be strong in the process of losing someone. Learn to let go and face your emotions. Remember, even Jesus wept.

Day 31 - Expectancy in Rest

Psalm 8:3; 9:1-2; 104

Expectancy and emotions go together. There's always excitement when there is something to look forward to! What do you do when life slows down and kids leave home? You and your spouse are left at home alone. Sometimes you can even be without your spouse. Many have seen me as a busy person, always on the go,and loving every minute of it.

Today I decided to walk down to the park in Ozark, MO. The Finley River seem to be glowing with ripples as the wind captured the reflection of the sun, and there were little boys throwing rocks in the water. As the green grass contrasted against the blue sky, I knew it was a beautiful day. I was amazed new discovery began to unfold. I began to notice more details as my Father's creation began to unfold before me. He was teaching me to enjoy life and learn to smell the roses.

If you are busy all the time, maybe it's time to take in the scenery and rest in what He has created. Have expectancy in the place of rest away from the rush and you will be glad you did!

Day 32 - Testing Will Come

Isaiah 41:10-13; James1:2-4

I never liked the times of testing, but I have also learned over the years that it's a good thing. As testing produces character, your weakness will also be exposed. It's difficult to improve your weakness if you are always focusing on your strengths. I believe our Father wants us strong in all areas of our lives. We see weakness as weakness, while God sees it as His strength. We are not made to go on the road of life by ourselves, and that is why we need our Heavenly Father's strength. Our flesh never likes weakness, but to our spirit, it's a chance to grow stronger in Him. I know He is pleased with our natural abilities when we are doing the right thing, but He is also pleased in our inabilities as we grow stronger in Him. He sees our weakness as opportunities for Him to take our hand and walk us through life's problems.

Think about this next time you have trials and you feel like you are failing in them. Just take it easy! Take a hold of His hand. He is waiting to take you through the hardest places of your life. He is your strength and refuge!

Day 33 - Reality of the Spiritual World

Psalm 37:1-27

In many areas of our lives, we may have something new to learn from the spiritual realm. These lessons can be very unusual and not make sense in the natural realm. For example, things that have gone on beyond our control. Have you ever said, "How in the world did I ever get myself in this situation?" You may be in situations right now where you may be experiencing pressure from every side. The Holy Spirit may say, "Do you trust me?" This is not a fun place to be, but when based on prayer and trust, it can be the safest place. Some people may be out of the will of God, which is causing Father God to do some pruning in our lives. Keep in mind that fruit trees may bear more fruit after being pruned.

You can see God moving in mysterious ways. It's good to see our Father reaching His hand down and moving things beyond our control. Looking back, I have to chuckle as I see what went on behind the scenes in many situations in the spiritual realm.

Let the Spirit of God bring you to a place to learn to trust Him even when you can't see it with your natural man.

Day 34 - Weeds and Seeds

Matthew 13:18-30

I like to garden because it's so much fun to plant things and see them grow. I think I got the green thumb from my mom. When I was younger we worked in the vegetable garden together. I really didn't like it at first, but I learned to enjoy it when I saw the end results.

My mom left behind a lot of unlabeled seeds after she passed away, and I inherited them. A friend of mine came over one day and we decided to plant them in seedling containers. We had a Later I observed my seeds growing what looked like blades of grass, while others looked like flowers. Some were small and delicate while others were big and strong. I think birdseed was mixed in the dirt.

My Heavenly Father began to speak to me about all of this. He was saying people are like the seeds. Don't judge them because you don't know if they are weeds or flowers. He told me some are fragile and some are delicate, while others are strong and grown up in their spirit. He told me to never give up on people. Your enemy can become your friend with the help of the Holy Spirit.

Be careful how you judge your weeds and flowers. Make room for them to grow!

Day 35 - Are You Teachable?

Isaiah 60:4-19

A teachable spirit is something we should all try to achieve. Not everyone likes to be told what to do, however if they would open themselves up to listening, they could learn a lot. Constructive criticism is actually a good thing if you know how to take it.

The stress comes in when we resist change. Being flexible s a great blessing. Getting locked into a mindset can bring grief to yourself and others as well. Have you ever heard the old saying, "You are as stubborn as an old mule?" Stubbornness is a mindset that stems from pride, and you can potentially make really bad decisions. Common sense can go out the door.

Wisdom and self-control can out wit any form of stubbornness. Be flexible and use wisdom! Move in change and stubbornness will go.

Day 36 - Love Beyond Measure

Psalm 103

One day I asked Father God for a desire of my heart while out walking. It went something like this: "I know you gave my niece a horse, and if you did that for her I know you can do that for me. If you really love me, then have someone give me a horse." I knew that He loved me, but I really was having a, "could I have that too" kind of day. I was frustrated. After asking then I thought, "I wonder if I should not have said that?" So I said, "Well if you don't want to give me a horse, that would be okay."

Two weeks later at a meeting at church I asked my friend, "How is your horse. Did you get involved with Cowboys for Christ yet?" Late, she said that God put it on her heart to give me her horse if I asked those two questions.

The day came to see my horse, but I just knew I couldn't keep him. I told my prayer to my friend that gave me the horse, and she told me her prayer as well. For her to give me her horse was like Abraham sacrificing Issac on the altar, but the ram was provided instead. For me I could see His awesome hand of love. We both were amazed at the workings of our Father in our lives. I gave her horse back, and was in awe at what had happened.

Never question the love of your Father. He loves you so much and He just might show it to you in a way that you don't even realize!

Day 37 - Steering Right or Left

Psalm 143:5-12

Have you ever seen people go from one extreme to another? I have and it seems like the difference between day and night. Sometimes certain things make people do that. Mostly they will stabilize back to the middle with the right circumstances. Getting off balance can be dangerous to our health and well-being. Often it's our emotions. We all face times of imbalances, especially during hard times or when tragedies happen. It's comforting to know that no matter what, our Heavenly Father is always stable. If we are hearing correctly from the Holy Spirit, we can receive His strength during these times. Sometimes our hearing can get muffled by the noise and busyness of the world. That is when it is good to have a heart-to-heart talk with the Father. If you find yourself going from one extreme to another it's time to sit with your Heavenly Father for His wisdom and counsel. Stay grounded in the word.

He will give you balance as you need it. It's your job to ask for it!

Day 38 - Spare Parts

Exodus 23

I'm amazed at the patience and talent it takes to put a new engine in a vehicle. I've also seen the extra parts that have been left over. I'm thinking, "I hope that vehicle is safe to go down the interstate at 70 miles an hour!"

Have you ever thought about that in your personal life? Its like trying to go from A to D and missing B and C. In reality, we all want to get from A to Z and into our "promised land" as soon as possible. A lot of steps that the Lord is taking you on, may seem to go nowhere. Believe me, there is a purpose in everything God does. He may keep you at a certain step until you get the lesson because He is teaching you. I wouldn't want to drive in the half put together vehicle where all the parts are left on the floor. Later you could have a wreck from all the missing parts. It's better to stay put rather than to adventure ahead on your own. Think about that when you want to skip God's lessons in life. Do you want to have a spiritual wreck later? It's good to know you can trust Him no matter what the steps are!

Be patient and faithful and you will get to your personal "promised land!"

Day 39 - Steady in Your Follow Through

Luke 5:1-11

Have you ever wondered why some people seem to have an easy life while others seem to struggle in their finances? I think a lot of that comes from not having a good follow-through. I have seen a lot of people just give up right before they reach the end of the rainbow with the pot of gold. What about the disciples when they fished all night and didn't have any fish? Jesus told them to cast their nets to the other side. Of course they caught so many fish that it started to sink their boat. They even had to get other boats because their bounty of fish was so huge from their obedience.

Next time you feel like quitting, ask the Father, "what do I need to do?" Remember you may be right on the verge of your breakthrough. He wants us to prosper! He wants us to win! Keep steady in your follow through!

Day 40 - Giants in the Land

1Samuel 17:32-51

We all have giants we have to face. They are the problems too big for us to handle. It's in that time courage comes in. It may be that the giant is your money problem. That is when wisdom is needed. No matter what situation you're facing, the solution is always there.

David was given an over-sized suit of armor to fight the giant. His armor was so big that he could hardly move. The world will try and solve your problems like that silly armor. We need the courage and wisdom of the Lord to face our giants. We need to stand up and use the strategies and words the Lord is giving us. Then, and only then, will we be able to slay our giants.

Stand strong in the Lord and the power of his might!

Day 41- Keeping Solid in the Time of Testing

Luke 8:20-25

It seems we go through a lot of steps in times of testing. We have to find that place where God wants us. When we are sure of our purpose, sometimes distraction can come our way.

Fear began to take control of the disciples when they saw the waves and their boat was sinking. As they realized they needed help, their calls became urgent! Jesus spoke to the storm, and His action of peace came in the form of a declaration. Peace came and the storm ceased because of what He spoke.

What are the fears in your life? Do you need to step out of your boat? Have you reached your destiny? You may have gone through the tough times and have weathered a lot of storms. Many of us go through times of testing. The truth of your success is whether you will keep trying and not give up!

Step into your boat of destiny and weather the storms of life! You are not alone. The Lord will help calm the storms of your life!

Day 42 - Team Players

Philippians 2:1-11

From time to time I watch different sports events. A well put-together team can win. I've also watched hotshot players. Everyone gives them the ball, and they're always the ones to make the critical play and point. However, I've observed when that person gets hurt the team can go downhill fast. It would be much better for that team to know how to utilize each player and operate with teamwork.

In God's Kingdom, we need to know what it means to be a team player. You may be the best pastor or the best singer, but are you developing team players for His Kingdom? Everyone needs to be given a chance to grow in His kingdom. Let's face it--we can't all do everything ourselves. We need each other. The churches need each other, and ministries need each other too. You may be at work, but are you a team player?

Whether you are a mentor or being mentored, start planning to be a team player, and watch His Kingdom flourish!

Day 43 - Get out of the Rut

Ephesians 5:13-15

Many times our lives change because of a lack of planning or tragic circumstances. Some people seem to get in a rut and even stay there. In doing this, you have two choices. You can accept your rut, or do something about it. It takes boldness to move out of the rut,and often it takes a different plan of action. You need to change something. Seize a plan. You start by asking God, "how?" Ask Him to bring opportunities to you and start looking for them. Grow in wisdom and the knowledge from Him. Step out of the boat of your comfort zone. Get in the realm of God's zone. Think like your Heavenly Father thinks. You may ask, "How does He think?" We may think of impossibilities while He thinks of possibilities. He sees potential in our lives before we even see it. Don't sell yourself short! God sees the bigness of His creation in you!

Step out of that rut! Get up and be strong! He is waiting on you to step out!

Day 44 - Entrapped Mind

Romans 12:1-3; Ephesians 4:22-24; Colossians 3:1-10

How many times have you let the enemy trap your mind by thinking you can't accomplish what the Lord wants you to do? It's time to take possession of our King's money system. We need to position ourselves in doing bigger things for God. If the enemy can keep you in "small mind set" thinking, he can then stop the "big God" thinking of destiny for you. You may have sowed and sowed and have not seen the growth You may lack wisdom and knowledge. When God brings us opportunities, do we cringe and freeze up because of what we have to accomplish? For years I've asked God, "How do I get the money for all the things you want me to do?" I never felt comfortable asking for a handout when God has given me a creative mind and strong hands to do the work. We have to step out in faith and do the work. My husband and I began to see opportunities that helped us grow, expand, and think differently. With this new mind set, God began to line up divine connections. It all started with our mind set change and willingness to move forward.

Don't live in poverty thinking! Let your God - given dreams out and begin believing and doing!

Day 45 - Mind of the Drifter

Psalm 94:19; 2 Corinthians 10:4-5; Philippians 4:7

Have you ever thought that you don't belong, and you are an outsider? Many people in the body of Christ feel that way. Some feel isolated and alone. Some want to hide in their hurt, but the pain won't go away. Are you like that? It will cause you to drift further and further away from your brothers and sisters in Christ. The enemy wants to separate you from the body and then from your Heavenly Father. Don't fall for that! Violently take action against that situation! Start confessing that you are valuable to the kingdom of God. You have something that people need in His body. When you begin to think differently and confess things differently,that is when things begin to change. Soon you can look back and see that the old drifter thoughts are gone.

Remember to resist the enemy and he will flee! Take captive of what you think, because you have the mind of Christ!

Day 46 - Excess Baggage

Corinthians 2:6-16

Sometimes God wants to pour things in us, but He can't because we have too much excess baggage. How many times as parents have you ever wanted to give your children something? You may want to but are aware your children won't be able to handle it. We would have an overload if God gave us everything we think we need. Instead, God wants to give us wisdom along with other things. He may delay answering our prayers in some of our life priorities. Circumstances often don't change for a reason. Your Heavenly Father Knows everything you need. Why not ask Him if there is anything in your life that you are carrying around like excess baggage? Is there anything you want to pour into me?" Let Him speak to you and be ready to listen.

He wants to be able to take the bad and pour in the good! Let's be ready for change!

Day 47 - Communication Galore

Romans 8:12-17

   Have you ever had a one-sided conversation with someone when you can't seem to get a word in edge-wise? You may have something important to tell them, but their mouth and mind won't let you say anything. When you do get a chance to express yourself, they are in a locked mindset and won't even listen to you.

   We all know that God wants to talk to us, so we can all have the opportunity to hear from Him. Here is an example to help you understand His voice. When mom has fresh-baked cookies she will say, "Stay out of the cookie jar, it will spoil your supper!" Can you just see that little boy reaching his hand up in the jar when his mom leaves the room? He will be hearing, "don't get in the cookie jar." That is how God can talk to us. He talks to us on a one-on-one level.

   Reading the Bible will help sharpen your ears to hear better. It will help you know the truth of what you hear. As you train your ears, your conversation will open up more to Him on a day-to-day basis. He is inside of you guiding you.

Let His heart speak clearly to you always! He wants with communicate to you   every day!

Day 48 - Be Strong and Have Courage

Psalm 46

Stepping out into new territory takes courage for most people. Fear is a territory stopper. Dealing with fear begins first in your heart by nature, and then it enters your head as you try and figure things out. Your heart can bring out the best in you when your heart is in Christ. So let Him be in control of your heart. Jesus overcame fear. When your heart is strong and fearless, a new challenge seems to take on a new prospective. You will only possess what your heart can process when the fear is out of the way.

Jesus overcame His fear of death because of His love for us. A lot of people lack motivation because they have no desire for commitment. Commitment comes from a determined desire to accomplish great things. Some people who are motivated to make money may get frustrated when the money doesn't come in. Sometimes it requires that the money that you may have invested to stay in one place for a longer period of time. That reserve of your money has to have a plan. That plan to produce money will only satisfy if you let your heart be lead by Christ.

Let Christ lead your heart! Bring out the best by stepping into His courage and strength!

Day 49 - Whole Heart

Matthew 22:37

My life changed for the better when my desires changed. The world tugs at your heart and pulls it in many different directions. I believe God wants all of your heart, not a small portion of it, but all. How can you embrace ministry if you haven't given Him your total heart? Yes, He will embrace the portion of ministry you give Him, but why not let Him have all of your heart? Don't worry, He won't overload you or mistreat you. He is a good Father, and He will lead you to green pastures for rest when you need it.

Every day is a ministry day when you give God your whole heart! Have a wonderful day serving our King!

Day 50 - Working in God's Food Chain

John 4:31-36

    Do you want to have a deep and effective impact on the world? Our Heavenly Father loves us just as much as He loves His Son, Jesus. Jesus loves His Father as well as us. Jesus was in His Father's plans when He came to die for us. The Heavenly Father placed everything in His hands, and because of that you have been grafted into our Heavenly Father's Kingdom. All authority is placed in our hands too! Verse 34 said that His food was to do the will of Him who sent me and to finish His work. Do you realize that the Spirit of God's unlimited anointing is dwelling in us? We have been given His power! Think about that the next time you have an unusually difficult situation!

Remember there's no limit in God's Kingdom. He wants you to do everything in the power of His Holy Spirit! We are His hands and feet!

Day 51 - Fishers of Men

Mark 1:16-20; John 21:1-6

There are people in the river of this life that are not yet caught. They have not really given their heart to the Lord all the way and don't have a personal relationship with Him. They have only waded in to see what it is like, but it will take you and me to catch them. Everything that you do can be in line to help catch them. Make sure your line has a hook on the end of it. Ask the Holy Spirit to help you use the proper bait. Make sure one ingredient is love. When we all work together, in love a net is formed. We can catch a lot of fish with it! That is how we can become fishers of men.

Build a team and let's catch some fish! Remember it takes patience and love!

Day 52 - River of God

Psalms 46:1-11; Ezekiel 47; Revelation 22:1-5

One song that comes to my mind is, "The River of God." One version goes like this; "the river of God sets my feet a dancing." What is the river of God? As I studied this, I found out that it's a place where God dwells. Ezekiel 47 says, "That where the river of God went there was life." The river contained life that the trees were bearing fruit all the time. The fruit was for food and the leaves for healing of nations. The water was so fresh because it came from the sanctuary of the throne of God and the Lamb. Wherever the river went, it brought life John 7:38 says, "Whoever believes in me, as the Scripture has said, streams of living water will flow from within him."

We are a conduit of that river through the Holy Spirit. We are to bring life where we go. When you flow out of the Holy Spirit, you bring the refreshing water of His Spirit.

Come and let His great river of life flow out of us!

Day 53 - Feeding the Sheep or Resting

Matthew 11:28-30

Sometimes in our personal life people go through stages of changes that never seem to end, even in business as well. We all need to take time to rest as well! Overworking yourself can get old. Even Jesus escaped into the mountains. He led His disciples to a place of rest. The Lord will never give you any more than you can handle, but sometimes we take on more than we should. Jesus said, "His burden is light," right? We are the ones who make choices that bring us stress. The other part of that verse says, "His yoke is easy." Are you carrying the load yourself? If the load is spiritual, let Jesus carry it. If it's physical, ask for some help. Some people don't get anyone to help them because they have not asked. It seems to me there is another verse about asking. "Ask and it shall be given to you," right? You might have a load to carry that the body of Christ can help you with.

Feeding the sheep can be weary and draining at times so a time of refreshing is necessary to work effectively in the Kingdom of God.

Make sure you have balance so you can keep on being a blessing to those who need you!

Day 54 - Serving with Love

John 13:1-17

I'm glad that Jesus demonstrated His love by washing His disciples feet. He did this service out of the act of love. Remember when you serve others, to do it out of the act of love. When we do things with a wrong heart it causes us to keep track, like a balance sheet, asking "what do I get for doing this?"

Jesus said if you want to be great in the kingdom be a servant of all. When you're serving out of love it takes all the stress out of it. The Holy Spirit loves to do things for others. Doesn't it make you feel good when you are doing things in love? When we feel like we have to do things it can cause stress in serving others. When we have to do things for others, why not think of each task as an act of love in love? It takes all the stress out of serving, and brings in that joy.

When you're serving others do it by serving in love! Think of it as serving your Heavenly Father!

Day 55 - Heart of a Lion

Isaiah 40:28-31; Luke 22:39-46

Most people have seen the movie Rocky. If you have not, Rocky lived in the Philadelphia slums, and he became a boxer. He had to work hard to become the underdog champion. Mick was his trainer. Rocky learned to fight from in his heart to win.

Life can be hard at times with circumstances and life issues that are overwhelming. Everything can be thrown at us at once. I have found that is the best time for me to grow and be strong. Have you ever wanted to run away from your problems? Problems will follow you around until you face up to the issues you are struggling with.

Having the heart of a champion like Jesus, the Lion of Judah. Think about what Jesus had to do. I Did He ever give up? No! In the garden of Gethsemane, His sweat was like blood. He had the Lion of Judah heart.

Our weakness is mostly within the mind. Thoughts come up like, "I can't possibly do that." We have to think differently. Our heart and mind have to think like a champion with the heart of a lion!

Let the spirit of the living God rise up within you to soar on winds of eagles. You can do it. Listen to hear your Heavenly Father cheering you on!

Day 56 - Take a Drink

Psalm 107:1-9

When you're thirsty, water looks refreshing and tastes the best. Spiritually speaking, when you are dry, that is when you need a drink from God's River. Dry and hungry people will come looking for refreshment. You aren't the only one that has dry seasons in your life. We all go through them. In times when this has happened to me, I would think, "Where have I gone wrong? I feel like I am not in love with the Lord? I don't have love or compassion for anyone." All of this kind of thinking is wrong. In fact, you are getting ready to have some very good times with the Lord! You're getting ready to dive in deep in the spirit of learning and teaching. You're getting ready to have passion like you have never had before!

Be encouraged when you feel like you are in the desert. Remember that flowers bloom in the desert too. You will find your oasis!

Day 57 - Taking a Leap of Faith

Hebrews 10:37; 11

Everybody crosses the bridge of decision at one time or another. It can suddenly alter your life. I have learned in times of great decision to ask for God's wisdom. Sometimes after seeking that wisdom you may need to take a leap of faith. If you could see where you are going you wouldn't need that stepping-out kind of faith. Faith is the substance that requires action. God wants us to learn how to step out. Some people live by fear and never step out. Some are trying to hear from God and they have learned to take that step of faith. Learning is a good thing. Sometimes we need to make decisions from our spirit. Other times we listen to Christians with good integrity who hear from Father God as well. In stepping out, God is teaching us. I believe listening to His voice is a process. It is always in God's plan for us to learn and grow even if we fall down. He will always pick you up. How can we lead if we don't first grow?

What are you waiting for? Step out and take that leap of faith!

Day 58 - See With the Spirit

John 7:24; Galatians 2:6

Things aren't always the way they seem to be. The issue of character always go deeper than just what you can see from the outside. People's eyes may have a fierce look to them, but they can be just as timid as can be. They try to look like something that they're not, but the true identity is inside of them. With spiritual maturity you can see inside them and be able to know them. You will know what kind of fruit is inside of them. You can ask God for wisdom. He will help you to not judge them but to know how to minister to them. When you can see what's inside of them, you're able to determine what they need. I love to minister to people, and when the Holy Spirit hits the target I can tell it is working. They may start crying, and things in their life comes forward that they are trying to overcome. I love it when I see the Holy Spirit minister to people, and watch the things that He unfolds in this life!

Don't look at the person from the outside. Look at them from their heart. That's the best way to minister!

Day 59 - Graveyard Mentality

Matthew 10:42

A lot of people think that when they're old they have no more reason to exist. I'm telling you there is so much to do within the kingdom of God. For one thing people can really pray. Our prayers count. It is always important to continually hear from God and then do what He says. I hope you choose to not just sit there and do nothing. We need to always be working for His Kingdom. It doesn't matter where the place is, or what situation we are in. We need to be able to do something for Him. You never retire in God's Kingdom. As we look up to Him, we don't want Him to look down and see a graveyard of people who don't think they matter much in life. Even a cup of water to a person in need is important.

Let us keep our ears open as well as our hearts! We have a big adventure, and it is not over until Jesus comes again or we are called home!

Day 60 - Mighty is the Hand of God

Psalm 34:3; 46:91; Proverbs 29:25; 1 John 4:18

We live in a world today where people are really scared of the future. The Lord says to not have fear because fear is of the enemy. Jesus is perfect, and His love casts out all fear if you trust the love that He has for you. If you do that, you won't be scared of anything that can come your way. I have seen people go to so many extremes to prepare for the future. They don't have the hope in Christ Jesus. They will put their hope in other things like their own well-being. Someday, whether Jesus comes again, or you simply die, you have to face that time. I believe Jesus wants us to watch, pray, and wait. He also wants us to continue to do the things that we need to do. He wants us to continue to go forward with our lives. We should not put our trust on a certain date of when that will happen. We need to be busy in the kingdom! Never stop doing the work of the Lord!

We need to look up, and continue to touch the lives of people.

Day 61 - Shoulder to Lean On

Psalm 68:18; Matthew 11:28-30

The problem some people have is they take on too many things without the needed help. Jesus wants us to have His shoulders to lean on. It will give you so much peace. All that energy that we take upon ourselves is hard to deal with. I found that when I'm leaning on Him I have a better understanding of what is happening in my life. I then know the things that I need to do that day, and I see the opportunities that come my way. I can also be content with what I have because He is there with me. I can have peace even if I have a lack. I know everything comes from the Lord.

It's time to lean on Him! He gives you a sense of peace that you never had before.

Day 62 - Marching Order Day

Romans 8:5 and 14; John 10:25-27

There are times in my life when I am really adamant about getting something done. It's like I cannot get it past my mind. The Holy Spirit keeps bringing things to us for a reason. It may be somebody we need to pray for. The Lord will continually bring them or a particular situation to our heart. When He does that, it is often the time when He wants to get something accomplished. It might be something in the kingdom market place. Just think of what you need to get done. But not every day is a ministry day. He wants us to enjoy our day of rest. It is part of our responsibilities to do things to take care of ourselves. God gives each one of us responsibilities for ourselves and others. When we take care of of our personal responsibilities, it can free up our time. Then we will be able to help somebody else

---

Let's not put off what we can do today! You never know what He might have you do tomorrow.

Day 63 - Shaking

Galatians 5:22; Ephesians 5:8-13

   As I was praying one morning for the body of Christ. God began to show me that shaking is coming to the body. The shaking is a good thing. Do you want to have bad fruit on your tree? Think about an apple tree when the ripe fruit begins to rot if not picked. Usually rotten fruit will fall to the ground when an apple tree is shaken. Occasionally good fruit will fall as well. The rotten fruit is left while the ripe fruit is picked. Have you ever had your fruit tree picked? I'm talking about the fruit of the Spirit. When your tree is shook what comes off your tree? Is it ripe or rotten fruit? When things aren't going right and you're in a desperate situation, make sure you are displaying good fruit.

   Let's have good fruit of the spirit manifest in times of testing. They will know us by our fruit. Let's draw nonbelievers to us by our good tasting fruit!

Day 64 - Desperate for Him

Psalm 91:1-2; Matthew 6:33; Hebrews 11:2; John 4:23-24

I'm just too busy. That's what a lot of people say when it comes to spending time with the Lord. When He has your undivided attention, it is a special time for Him and you. This is when I focus on nothing but Him. There are times that He will draw me away, and I go to pray for something specific and urgent. You can spend time in prayer driving or walking, but beware of occasional distractions. Pray often, the outcome can change your life. Be desperate to take Him with you every day and everywhere. When was the last time you began to just thank Him for everything He has given you? It's a time to honor Him, worship, and thank Him. Clear your mind of your agendas and just focus on Him. If you are not used to doing this it may seen difficult at first. You will see the tremendous value in it as you keep having a conversation with Him. You will have the edge you need and the peace. It will give you confidence and you will see the big picture and purpose for your life!

Be desperate for Him and He will change your life for the better!

Day 65 - Grave Clothes

Romans 8

Many times, as we go about our busy day, we need to have our grave clothes on. Death is not an easy thing, yet Paul says, "I die daily." The death I'm talking about is death to self and the flesh nature. We need to be alive in Christ. Our will can be strong in us. It tends to go in our own direction and not in God's direction. Our ways may affecting others if we are not following what Christ wants us to do. We need to be reminded constantly that we should have our grave clothes on throughout the day. Nobody likes the dying part of this message, yet everyone likes being alive in Christ.

Ask the Holy Spirit to remind you to have your grave clothes on. So let's be alive in Christ!

Day 66 - Mission Impossible

Isaiah 12:2; Proverbs 24:5; Philippians 4:12-13

We all have challenges in life. Some things maybe easy for us, but hard for others. In the Bible we read, "I can do all things through Christ." Some things require our effort, but after doing them for a while, they might become easier. What about the things we know we could achieve but lack drive or ambition? Most things that require effort are not impossible to do. Applying effort is the big key to success. You have to say to yourself, "do I really want to do this?" Our attitude is what can make them the "mission impossible." Sometimes we make things hard or easy because we wrestle with them in our mind. If God is wanting you to do what you think is impossible, think again. Don't be discouraged. Take one step at a time. Get a plan together. You can do it!

Let's just get busy and do it. You will see the results soon.

Day 67 - Increase With Measure

Proverbs 24:5; Mark 9:41; Luke 17:5-6; Roman 12:7; 1Thessalonians 3:12-13; 2 Thessalonians 1:3; 2 Peter 1:3-10

You can never go wrong by giving. You can never out give the Giver. Our Heavenly Father requires increase from us. We need to increase our joy in a sad world. We need to increase our hope in a hopeless world. Increase our love for each other. Increase our finances as well. Do you understand what I'm getting at? Increase in everything. When people think of giving, they think of money. Let me challenge you to give in a new way. Give your time to somebody. Give a smile or a kind word or gesture. Give in a way that only you can give. How about give in character?

Let Him tell you some areas in your life that you need to increase with measure!

Day 68 - Planning Your Future

Proverbs 14:22-27; Jeremiah 29:11-13

Many people plan for the future in their businesses. They set goals for the New Year. How many plan and set a goal with God? Now that I have you thinking, what goal could you set right now? Today I was just drawn away with Him. It's a private intimate time with my beloved future Bride Groom. The first thing He said to me is, "I've been missing you." I know that He walks with me all the time. I know He was referring to our personal time alone with no distractions. What is the best time for you to spend personally alone with him? I know we all get busy, but we all need this. It's so worth it! Could you find a better investment time?

Put Him in your planner! That is the best plan you can have!

Day 69 - Make It Joy

Psalm 68:3-6; Psalm 100

People experience tragedy, but it's up to us to bring out the joy. Joy is what gives us strength. It gives us a reason to live. Nobody can bring out your joy but you. Many people who are hurt tend to just trap their joy inside of them. Joy can bring out the best in us when we let it out. Try humming a tune. It's amazing how that will make you feel better. The expression of you giving a sound of joy can be contagious. Don't you like being around joyful people?

So what are you waiting for. Bring out your joy today! Ask the Lord to help you to bring your joy into people's lives today!

Day 70 - Is Devil is Attacking Me?

2 Corinthians 10:3-6; James 4:1-7; 1 Peter 5:8-9

Sometime when people are in a rut, they think the devil and demonic powers are after them. The truth is they have entertained the thought in their mind that the attack is from Satan and his demons. It really can comes from the choices they have been making. Here are some examples: my car is breaking down, the washer quit working, my kids are having relationship problems, no money for groceries, gas is too high, and so forth. None of this has to do with demonic powers. Cars break because of wear and tear. You may not have maintained it properly. The same is true with the washing machine. The kids may be doing something that makes other kids tease. The money problem could be from not educating yourself or being plain lazy. Find a way to fix your problems. When you research your problems, you will find answers to them. You will find out it's not the devil, after all. Flesh nature is most of our problem, which means we are the problem. When you feel like you are being attacked, find who the true culprit is. Quit giving the enemy any glory!

The Bible says to resist the devil and he will flee. Do not invite him in by claiming he is your problem!

Day 71 - Price and Value

Genesis 23; Psalm 16

Abraham had a need. Sarah died, and Abraham had no place to bury her. So he asked to buy a cave. The owner just gave him the cave and a field to bury the dead. He got it for free, and yet Abraham offered to pay full price for it. He gave it value by doing that. Very interesting. What a lesson in value. How many people would do that? Too many people want a hand out without even asking for a price.

Psalm 16 is another placement of value. David took refuge in God. He knew that he needed Him and couldn't do anything alone. He took counseling in God. He said that God is his right-hand. He had joy and happiness in that. The eternal pleasure was his happiness. Wow! How can we get to that point in our lives? Money does have value, but what you have in the Holy Spirit has more value.

So where is your value-money? Let's choose the Lord and use money as a tool in His kingdom!

Day 72 - What Matters Most

Philippians 4:1-9

I had one of those mornings when I didn't really want to get out of bed. I started thinking about my old dogs of the past, and how it affected me and other people when they died. I stopped myself and thought, why am I thinking about this? How do I quit thinking about this sad thought? Then the Holy Spirit brought to my mind the verses in Philippians. So that is what I'm going to think about. I began to think of church people who go to Sunday morning church. Many are happy to be there and enjoy the worship service and other things. Then the Holy Spirit said to me that very morning when I wake up needs to be like Sunday morning. Every fellow believer needs to make every day as a Sunday morning. They need to make it in their heart to have an "I love to worship Him" kind of day. Just do what matters the most! Today have an "I love you Heavenly Father" kind of day!

Let that explosive love for Him explode on to others!

Day 73 - Sweet Inside and Out

Psalms 119:97-104

Some of the most sweetest times for me, have been when I let the Bible change me. The Holy Spirit gives you that desire for extra sweetness. I remember in high school when I decided to read the whole Bible in a year. The book of Proverbs changed me. I began to be more compassionate. My attitude began to change. I saw things differently as if I was putting a new pair of glasses on.

I remembered this half blind albino girl in high school that everyone teased, and my heart was enlarged. I began to be kind to her. In P.E. class, no one picked her to be their partner, but I did. When I did, my PE teacher noticed. She called me in her office one day to ask me why I didn't go out for sports. I told her that I had to work. She wanted to reward me somehow for being physically fit as well and my attitude to work with anyone in P.E. Because of that, on awards night, I received a special award they created just for me. I was a junior in high school when I received that award for the first time. No other person in 9th through 12th got it but me, and I was so honored to get it. I knew it was because of my changed heart from reading the Bible.

Let the sweetness of His word change your attitude. You never know what may happen!

Day 74 - Private Investigator

John 3:19-21

Have you ever had people want to know and see everything about you? They give you that look that seems to say, "I want to know more." I wonder what reflection they will see if they will look at you? Are you like honey to a bee, a warm person drawing them in, or a self centered one that repels them away?

We are to mirror Christ in the Holy Spirit. What comes out of us is what people see. You can never hide the truth. If you are angry, it will come out by your actions. How many people enjoy being around an angry person who explodes often? Do you want to know the secret that draws people to you like a magnet? It's the power of the Holy Spirit acting in your life. The Holy Spirit knows what people need. He can convey the message of Jesus to that person by the way they act. The key is the heart that comes from within us. Each person has a mirror of the Holy Spirit from within. Have you mirrored Him today?

Let's draw people by the way of the Holy Spirit into His kingdom. Let them be our private investigator!

Day 75 - Character

Proverbs 11:20; Matthew 7:15-20; 12:33-37; James 3:17

The Lord showed me that people often judge others by their character. Sometimes that judging of character can be misguided because we haven't really known them very long. I think if you pray and ask God for wisdom, He will give you the understanding. I know what the Bible says about not judging people, but it doesn't say anything about judging the fruits of their character. We need to know who we are working with. Sometimes we won't see the true colors of a person's character right away. People have a tendency to cover up their character flaws in so many ways. Only God can see their true character and go down into the very core of their spirits. He can also let us know if they're the right relationship match for what we need in our business or other areas of our life.

Holy Spirit to give us wisdom when it comes to hiring and what we see in people. We can discern their character as we inspect their fruit.

Day 76 - Act of Love

Matthew 10:40-42

Love is an action word. Some acts of love require time. Time is a value given to you each day. To a homeless person, a nursing home resident, kids out on the street, the widows and the elderly, the present time is so much in their minds because they have needs now. Many people say they can love these people. How can you love these people? Can you give your time to them? It's easy to say I love you, but love is an action word. What have you done to love any of them? How can you love them in the future? I have found that planning takes action to get that job done. Perhaps you can plan an outing with them. Just plain listening to them can say I love you. Every day can be the same for them. Many times they live for the moment of that day. What are some areas you can take action to love someone like that?

Love is an action word so make every day count!

Day 77 - Growing Season

Isaiah 49:1-26

The Lord wants us to be His mouthpiece. We need to speak out His blessing and favor. Fruit grows on trees, and when it is ripe, it tastes sweet. We have the fruit of the Holy Spirit. Are you letting them taste your fruit tree? Time will tell what the maturity of the fruit is on your tree. Sow life into people you see. If they are thirsty, give them a drink from the refreshing waters of the Holy Spirit. Some people are depressed, so bring joy to them. Take time to help them grow.

I want to challenge you today and every day, to always speak and act out of the fruit of His Spirit!

Day 78 - Better to Give than Receive

Act 20:32-35

For generations people have been wondering what makes people tick. Why do people act the way they do? Greed and money will cause people to make the most life altering decisions. Some have been poor and refused to change their life. Others change their outcome and say, "I don't want to be like that or live that way anymore." Many things in life are given to us as gifts or an inheritance. Some people fear moving forward financially so it keeps them from stepping out. Some give up on life and are stuck in the dullness of life.

I say we need to be a bright light. Jesus wants us to be a reflection of Him. We need to act like Him and have purpose like Him. It's never too late to change our destiny. Have His attitude because He is never down or gives up. Money or greed had no hold on Him, and He was not lacking either. Learn to give, and it will get better. If you have no money, you can give your heart. Small things can mean a lot to people. A smile and listening ears cost you nothing. March forward and be a giver. It will take the pressure off of you. You will feel better!

Give something today in ways that only you can give! Give yourself!

Day 79 - Bright Shiny Star

Philippians 2:12-18

A shining star of hope is what we need to become. A gift that keeps on giving. The word of hope can cost effort for some. We should not complain when life is not going well. I don't know about you, but I get hit by a brick every time I hear that! I sometimes run myself into the ground from working too hard, and when that happens I can get tired and grumpy. Who wants to be around arguing, complaining people anyway? So if you want to shine for Jesus, then shine and don't complain and argue. I love to be around people who are happy. Why not give that a try this week or even this month? Let's just make it a new habit!

Let us be that shining light and bring the word of life to people. True happiness comes when we bring others up. Lift them up and give them a boost. So just shine on!

Day 80 - Doing Our Best

Colossians 3:22-25

Does Jesus bring out the best in you? It an awkward question that only you can answer because it is a discovery of truth and purpose. The truth is, we all have things in our lives that we need to discover. This next question may hurt some of you, but it is the truth. Do you do your best when working for someone? Never refrain from doing your best. Bring out that champion from within. His power is in us. All we need to do is give our best whenever the moment is a tough one.

Go back and examine those questions. Let His purpose in you come forth. Do your best, and He will do the rest to bring glory to God!

Be a good example for others as you do your best for Him!

Day 81 - Pursue Happiness

Psalms 68:3-10; Proverbs 15:13

Happiness is a choice. Many choose to not apprehend it, so they lose it. Have you ever been in a negative situation that you can't ignore, and dwelling on the problem carries you to the next level of irritation? Before long you are all stressed out, and you have no joy. Then you think about your mountain of problems to be moved, and they still stay. Sometimes happiness is confronting that mountain head on and facing your responsibilities. Choose to fight and not give up.

Happiness can also come in a job well done because you stuck to it, and you are wise enough to know when to quit. You should have happiness in everything you do with the right attitude. In any situation you need to put on that happy mode!

Don't worry, be happy! Make it your daily routine!

Day 82 - Climb that Mountain of Hope

Romans 5:3-5

What are my options when It seems that I have lost all hope? Most often hopelessness is in our own minds. It can cause us to lose out when the situation is far from hopeless. When we are in need of rest, we can get easily frustrated and then we lose hope of accomplishing anything.

A hopeless person have to believe that things can change, Because when we are down and out the One that lives inside of us isn't. When we are frustrated we need to take one step at a time and climb that mountain. Then the next day we go a little higher. Sooner or later that mountain of frustration has been realized, and we can accomplish something that we thought we couldn't.

We all need to encourage one another especially when we lose all hope. The encouragement we give might help someone to climb that mountain of challenges. The One that lives inside of us can bring that help.

Let "Hope is on the way" be our motto!

Day 83 - Satisfaction Glow

John 17:9-16; 2 Corinthians 3:7-18

It's nice to have a safe place in the arms of the only one you love. He that dwells with the Most High is in the safest place he could ever be. It's a place of not wanting anything. You have everything. It's a continual holding on to what is dear to you. It's a letting go of the past failures and disappointments to achieve the inner peace you desire. Loneliness seems to just go away. Life can be like a shattered mirror, but the One you love helps pick up the broken pieces and make it whole again.

Sometimes we are the ones that judge ourselves when we pick up that mallet that declares guilty or not guilty. The freedom that comes from the Father's love can free us from that guilt. The fire of the Holy Spirit that can be fanned, can then come to the people that need to feel the warmth of the Spirit. They will see the glow of the Father's love. In Christ we have all we need, and the Father's hands are spread wide to embrace His love.

Let Him feel you full of the Father's love to reflect that love today!

Day 84 - Move that Mountain

Psalm 73:23-28; 105:4; Philippians 3:12-14

The top of the mountain always seems the farthest when you look at it from the distance. When you get closer it is a lot bigger than you think.

That's the way things are in real life. From a distance things aren't so big, until you get closer to that mountain of problems then it can seem so huge. We are supposed to overcome the mountains in our life, not look at them from a distance. Things cannot be repaired or fixed if you don't get closer to the problem.

Take control of your life today! Face that mountain up close and overtake it. That will change your life and help you conquer your fears!

Day 85 - Thankful Heart

1 Chronicles 16:8-10; Psalms 95:2; 100; 107:1; 118:28-29; 1 Thessalonians 5:18

Enjoy raising children they can give you joy. Have you ever been thankful to take a bite of an apple? You can taste that succulent fruit in your mouth. How about a nice warm bath on a cold day? What about a stroll in the park on a nice summer day, or the day you said, "I do" to your sweetie?

So many things we take for granted. Time can go by so quickly and before long life, is over. I just want everyone to be thankful and savor the moments that God has given us. We need to tell God thank you for so many wonderful gifts He has given us. The fact is no matter where you are and what you're doing, you should be thankful for that day. Find the treasures along the way.

Be thankful to the Lord! Tell Him how much you appreciate all the things He has done for you!

Day 86 - Place of Heavenly Position

Matthew 6:19-21; Luke 12:32-34

Having a high position is what makes some of us secure, especially when hard work moves us up the ladder of success. Some people need that to feel important, and others need it to feel powerful.

How are you in positioning yourself with your finances? Have you thought and made a plan on where your money is going to go? It's not enough to try and stretch your money. That's okay for the here and now, but what about the future beyond the here and now? What about the Kingdom of God?

What would it be like to have no limitations on our finances? To get that way it takes a plan, to position ourselves for heavenly kingdom purposes. We need to think of treasures to lay up for heaven as well. For where your treasure is, your heart will be. Is your heart thinking of heavenly places?

Let's position ourselves for the future in our finances.
Let's take some action.
We can impact the Kingdom of God through our lives.

Day 87 - Fantasy

Proverbs 23:18; Jeremiah 29:11-13

Sometimes having a little with fantasy in life is fun, but he truth is fantasy can steal the joys of reality from you. It can substitute things that are not real and bring deception. Why is it that everyone likes fantasy? Why does everyone want to fantasize on things? I believe the reason for this is people have lost hope. They have lost vision and insight for what the future has. They can't see anything positive in their lives so "make-believe" brings immediate satisfaction to them. They are on a short rope of hope, living a false vision into fantasy land. No longer do they experience any drive for what they could do. They shelter the past hurts and pains within the realm of fantasy, hoping to make themselves feel good. In reality, they are robbing themselves of the future adventure that God has for them.

When you think of fantasy remember it creates a false identity. Live out your identity in the real world of hope for the future. Only you can do it!

Day 88 - X Marks the Spot

Psalms 9:9-10; 25:8-14

When God has a plan for your life, He reveals part of it to you. You may think you have all the answers, but He knows and sets your path. You may go in a direction that you think is right, but when you ask Him, He will order your steps in the right direction.

God wants to make Himself powerful in you. It takes both you and Him to go the right way. When I would take steps in the direction that I felt was right, I also discovered when I was off. Then I would pray about things, and sometimes the answer didn't come. He may be working something in me that I am not aware of, and it is probably for my good. So I walk out my steps in faith because I have prayed. It may seem bleak at times. Trust me, He knows what He is doing. Let Him mark the spot of where you should be in your life.

You may never know the steps you are taking are right. He knows the plans He has for you. You need to breakdown that barrier you have and trust Him. He sees the whole future and full perspective of your life!

Day 89 - Breaking the Gates

Deuteronomy 2:1-6; 6:1-2; Proverbs 20:24; Isaiah 48:1

Some may think that life is so hard. The truth is it may be a mindset. Freedom can only come when we realize what our full potential is. It is like breaking down the gates of what is uncomfortable.

Has anyone ever said something, that just stopped you in your tracks? Some things, negative people say can come from deep-seated problems that they have. They seem to splash the fire out of us. Don't let them put the fire out of what God has put in your heart. What He has been speaking to you, do it. Sometimes things change in mid-stream of what you're doing. Listen to the voice of the Holy Spirit and He will help you. Make sure you are not avoiding your current commitments during that time. When things shift directions, it maybe for a purpose.

Step out and break the gates of the unknown. Listen to His voice. You will know what to do!

Day 90 - Who Me

1 Peter 3:13-16

Have you ever been blamed for something you didn't do? I have, and fellow believers were behind it. I was at the place where they had already made up their minds as to the accusation against me. A place in that no matter what I said, it wouldn't have made any difference. After reading 1 Peter 3:13-16, I found out I was suffering for doing right. I decided to wait it out in prayer, and I watched God fight my battles. I watched in peace knowing it would be okay. Later my name was restored from slander and everything was made right.

Let the Lord strengthen you in times of suffering. Be gentle and let God fight your battles!